What's the Issue?

WHAT'S FAKE NEWS?

By Joyce Jeffries

Orange County Library System
146A Madison Rd.
Orange, VA 22960
(540) 672-3811 www.ocplva.org

KidHaven
PUBLISHING

Published in 2019 by
KidHaven Publishing, an Imprint of Greenhaven Publishing, LLC
353 3rd Avenue
Suite 255
New York, NY 10010

Designer: Andrea Davison-Bartolotta
Editor: Katie Kawa

Photo credits: Cover (bottom) WICHAI WONGJONGJAIHAN/Shutterstock.com; cover (top) Rawpixel.com/Shutterstock.com; pp. 4, 12 GaudiLab/Shutterstock.com; p. 5 (bottom left) George Rudy/Shutterstock.com; p. 5 (bottom right) Dragon Images/Shutterstock.com; p. 5 (top right, top left) Monkey Business Images/Shutterstock.com; p. 7 MANDY GODBEHEAR/Shutterstock.com; p. 8 Iain Masterton/Canopy/Getty Images; p. 9 catwalker/Shutterstock.com; p. 11 Bloomberg/ Getty Images; p. 13 MicrovOne/iStock/Thinkstock; p. 15 happymay/Shutterstock.com; p. 17 G. De Cardenas/Getty Images; p. 18 Paket/Shutterstock.com; p. 19 (top) Dmytro Zinkevych/ Shutterstock.com; p. 19 (bottom) Gorodenkoff/Shutterstock.com; p. 20 Sam Edwards/OJO Images/ Getty Images.

Library of Congress Cataloging-in-Publication Data

Names: Jeffries, Joyce author.
Title: What's fake news? / Joyce Jeffries.
Description: New York : KidHaven Publishing, 2019. | Includes bibliographical
    references and index.
Identifiers: LCCN 2017059288| ISBN 9781534525832 (library bound book) | ISBN
    9781534525849 (pbk. book) | ISBN 9781534525856 (6 pack) | ISBN 9781534525863 (ebook)
Subjects: LCSH: Fake news–Juvenile literature.
Classification: LCC PN4784.F27 J44 2018 | DDC 070.4/3–dc23
LC record available at https://lccn.loc.gov/2017059288

Printed in the United States of America

CPSIA compliance information: Batch #BS18KL: For further information contact Greenhaven Publishing LLC, New York, New York at 1-844-317-7404.

Please visit our website, www.greenhavenpublishing.com. For a free color catalog of all our high-quality books, call toll free 1-844-317-7404 or fax 1-844-317-7405.

CONTENTS

Making Up Stories

What important things are happening in the world today? In many cases, we find out the answer to that question by reading, watching, or listening to the news. Some people get their news by reading newspapers and magazines or watching television shows, while others get it on the radio or online.

People want to be able to trust that the news they're getting is true. However, there are some people who make up untrue news stories. This is called fake news. How can you spot a fake news story? Read on to find out!

Facing the Facts 🔍

A person who writes news stories is often called a journalist or a reporter.

4

News literacy is the ability to judge how trustworthy a news story is. It's a very important skill because it helps people tell the difference between a true news story and fake news.

Fact or Fiction?

News stories are supposed to be based in facts that have been checked and found to be accurate, or correct. Fake news stories are fiction, or stories that have been invented by a person instead of really happening. In some cases, fake news stories can have some facts in them to make them look more believable.

Fake news stories can be reports of rumors, or stories that are spread around without anyone being sure they're true. Even though the rumor might not be true, people begin to believe it when enough people spread it.

Facing the Facts

Some websites create fake news stories to be funny. These funny fake stories are known as parodies or satire. They're not meant to be seen as factual news reports, but if people don't look at the website closely, they might think they're reading real news.

Rumors can hurt people whether they're spread in person or online. Rumors about famous people and world events are sometimes presented as news. It's important to always check the **source** of a story to find out if what's being spread is true.

Sharing Fake News

Today, there are more ways to get and share news than ever before. However, that also means there are more ways to spread fake news. The most common way fake news is spread is through the internet.

Some websites have been set up just to post fake news stories. They look like proper news websites, so people believe the stories they see on them must be true. Another way fake news is spread is through **social media platforms** such as Facebook and Twitter. Social media allows people to easily share stories with others—even if the stories are fake.

8

Facing the Facts 🔍

As of 2017, 43 percent of Americans said they often get their news online.

Facebook is one social media platform that people use to share fake news stories. The head of Facebook, Mark Zuckerberg, is working to find ways to fight the spread of fake news.

9

Reporting from Russia

Sometimes journalists write what they think are facts, but they make a mistake or report something that they think is true but is shown to be false later. This isn't the same thing as a fake news story, which is a made-up story that is presented as true.

For example, during the months before the 2016 presidential election in the United States, many fake news stories were shared. Many of these fake stories were created and spread by people from Russia. Even after the election of President Donald Trump, Russians were still spreading fake news stories online to try to **divide** Americans.

Facing the Facts

Russians have also been **accused** of spreading fake news in other countries, such as the United Kingdom, France, Germany, and Spain.

The spread of fake news became a major part of the 2016 presidential race between Donald Trump and Hillary Clinton. Russians sometimes pretended to be Americans on social media platforms so people would be more likely to believe their fake news stories.

A Different Meaning

Most people use the words "fake news" to talk about stories that are purposely made up. However, some people have started using "fake news" to mean different things. Today, some leaders and other powerful people have started calling news stories they don't like "fake news." They often use this term for news reports that make them look bad.

When leaders use the words "fake news" in this way, it can make people confused about what's true and what's not. This is why it's important to only call news stories "fake" when they purposely spread lies.

Facing the Facts

American newspapers began using the words "fake news" in the late 1800s to describe untrue stories.

Fake News Is...	Fake News Isn't...
an untrue news story with no real facts	facts that someone doesn't like or doesn't agree with
a rumor that has no trustworthy source	a true news story that makes someone look bad
a purposely made-up story	a person's opinion that is backed up by facts
lies that are knowingly spread because someone thinks it's funny	parodies or satire that are clearly labeled as such

People are sometimes confused about what fake news is. This chart can help you decide if a report really is fake news or if someone is using that term incorrectly.

Creating Confusion

Confusion is one of the biggest problems caused by fake news. In a 2016 study, 64 percent of adults in the United States said fake news caused a lot of confusion about current events.

Although fake news leaves a majority of Americans feeling confused, that hasn't stopped some people from spreading it. The same study reported that 23 percent of U.S. adults shared a fake news story. However, 16 percent of people didn't know the news they were sharing was fake when they shared it.

Facing the Facts

As of 2016, 39 percent of Americans said they felt very **confident** in their ability to spot a fake news story.

Sharing fake news can make people upset over something that didn't actually happen.

15

No Trust in the News

Another problem caused by fake news is that groups of people have stopped trusting parts—or all—of the news **media**. This is especially true for young adults. As of 2016, only 10 percent of them said they placed a lot of trust in the national news media.

It's good to be on the lookout for fake news, but it's not good to believe all news is fake news. Most journalists want to help citizens learn the truth about important people and events. When people don't trust the news, they're less likely to become active and informed, or educated, citizens.

Facing the Facts

People in the United States generally trust local news reports more than national news reports.

News reports help citizens decide who and what to vote for. When people don't trust the news or trust fake news instead of facts, it can **affect** how they vote.

17

Spotting Fake News

How can you tell if a news story is fake? You can start by checking where it came from. Major newspapers, news magazines, and their websites and social media pages are generally trustworthy sources. However, it's good to check to see if the same facts can be found in more than one trustworthy source.

If you're not sure if a news source can be trusted, you should find out more about it. It's also good to find out who wrote or shared a news story to learn if they're known for spreading fake news.

Many spelling mistakes on a website and stories with no known author can be signs of fake news. It's good to have an adult's help when looking at news online.

Facing the Facts 🔍

Videos can be sources of fake news, too. They can be cut and the sound can be changed to make things up or leave out important parts.

19

Telling the Truth

As more real and fake news sources are created, understanding the differences between them is going to become even more important. Fake news can cause many problems, and incorrectly calling a real news story "fake news" can be harmful, too.

People around the world are working to stop the spread of fake news. It may seem like a problem that only adults can fix, but it's never too early to start learning the difference between fact and fiction. News literacy skills can help everyone!

Facing the Facts 🔍

In a 2017 study, half of all people between the ages of 10 and 18 said knowing about the news helps them feel ready to make a difference in their community.

WHAT CAN YOU DO?

Learn more about how to spot fake news.

Talk to adults about the difference between fake news and factual news.

Only share news if you know it's true.

Don't spread rumors online or in person.

Use the words "fake news" only when you're talking about a story that purposely spreads lies.

Check the facts when you see a news story to make sure it's true.

Telling the truth isn't just an important part of the news. It's an important part of life, too. These are some ways to practice finding out the facts and sharing the truth instead of fake news.

GLOSSARY

accuse: To blame.

affect: To produce an effect on something.

confident: Having a feeling of belief that you can do something well.

divide: To separate into different groups.

media: The systems and ways of communication that are used to inform a large number of people.

social media platform: Websites and applications, or apps, that allow users to interact with each other and create online communities.

source: Someone or something that gives what is needed.

FOR MORE INFORMATION

WEBSITES

Binky's Facts and Opinions

pbskids.org/arthur/games/factsopinions/index.html

This game helps players learn what's a fact and what's an opinion.

Spotting Fake News

kids.nationalgeographic.com/explore/ngk-sneak-peek/april-2017/fake-news/

This website offers tips for spotting fake news and has a link to a test you can take to see how good you are at it.

BOOKS

Jennings, Brien J. *Fact, Fiction, and Opinions: The Difference Between Ads, Blogs, News Reports, and Other Media.* North Mankato, MN: Capstone Press, 2018.

Levete, Sarah. *Fakes and Hoaxes.* New York, NY: Gareth Stevens Publishing, 2017.

Mooney, Carla. *Asking Questions About How the News Is Created.* Ann Arbor, MI: Cherry Lake Publishing, 2016.

INDEX